Hands & Wings

Since 1985 **Freedom from Torture** (Registered charity no. 1000340) has been the only human rights charity dedicated solely to the rehabilitation and support of torture survivors seeking protection in the United Kingdom. It does this primarily through providing psychological and physical therapies; forensic documentation of torture; as well as practical, legal and welfare assistance for helping survivors to recover and begin to rebuild their lives.

The charity has five centres around the country staffed by full and part-time staff, plus many volunteers. Each year Freedom from Torture provides treatment for more than 1,000 people from around 80 countries across the world. Shockingly, the use of torture continues and with the growing number of refugees fleeing torturing states, the number of survivors who need support to rebuild their lives after suffering unimaginable trauma is increasing.

We are extremely grateful to Dorothy Yamamoto for presenting us with the idea and compiling the poems and to the poets who have freely contributed their work. We would like to thank Philip Pullman who has generously supported the book by writing the Foreword and helping us with the launch. Our gratitude for their help and support also goes to our sponsors, Henmans Freeth and Turpin & Miller, and particularly Blackwell's Bookshop in Oxford.

For more information about the organization's work visit www.freedomfromtorture.org

All proceeds from the sale of this book go to Freedom from Torture. In an attempt to meet the growing demands for their services they rely on the generosity of their donors so that they can try to reach out to as many survivors of torture as possible. By buying this book, you are supporting the invaluable work done by Freedom from Torture and contributing to their vision of a world free from torture. We thank you for your interest and support.

Freedom from Torture Oxford Supporters Group, 2015

Hands & Wings

Poems for Freedom from Torture

edited by

Dorothy Yamamoto

with a Foreword by Philip Pullman

White Rat Press 2015

First published in 2015 by

White Rat Press
114 Abingdon Road
Oxford OX1 4PZ

Cover design by Dan Cooper

Printed by StroudPrint
Lightpill, Stroud, Gloucestershire GL53 3NL
www.stroudprint.co.uk

Further copies may be ordered from Freedom from Torture
www.freedomfromtorture.org

from Ann Gibson
anngibsontc@btinternet.com

or from White Rat Press
www.whiteratpress.co.uk

ISBN 978-0-9933964-0-3

Foreword

Torture is the worst thing human beings can do to one another. The world has plenty of ways to make us suffer—illness, accident, mortality itself; but the deliberate infliction of pain is worse than any of these, because behind it lies malice. When suffering is willed, it seems to come from a depth of evil that illness and accident and death never plumb. Any attempt to help its victims is worth supporting.

So this anthology would deserve our attention whatever the quality of the contents. But as it happens, it's also worth reading for its own sake, because there are many fine poems here, and many distinguished poets. I was particularly struck by the number of pieces that show a close observation of the natural world, and a skill in depicting it. What the best poetry does is to show us analogies and let us interpret them ourselves, and there are many analogies in nature for human events, birth, love, sorrow, death . . . Death is very well seen here, in several poems that look at it clearly and closely and tenderly.

And I was glad to see a muntjac deer turning up in more than one poem. Earlier this year I was mowing a hayfield when the largest hare in the world leapt up in the middle of the unmown grass, and saw me and moved away, and as it reached the edge of the cut grass it turned into a muntjac and trotted towards the hedge, into which it vanished like mist, without rustling a single leaf. If I were a poet I'd do something with it, but I'm not. I did recognize, though, in several poems here, the same sudden irruption of wonder at the strangeness of a world that had such things in it.

And again and again, empathy: the sense of another human heart beating. That is the finest antidote to the cast of mind that makes torture possible. We shall never eliminate cruelty altogether, but every poem here shows that it's not inevitable, that human beings can feel and see and think in harmony with one another. Poetry is the sound of that happening.

Philip Pullman

Contents

AFAM AKEH

His story

Like parting folk at a travel lounge
we scan through memory
selecting stories like occasional dresses.
We fill the moment with talk but keep it light.

We talk food and talk sports, time ourselves
by the heaving of his chest as if on cue
to stop when it does. We record every stir
not sure what turn may mark the moment.

Silence is the monster. It stands Goliath-tall
against plea and plan, cheapening everyone:
against question, against mediation,
against our love of flowers and frontiers.

We watch our silent friend and talk.
We breathe. He still breathes.
We make a pact of that, fill up with air
and give voice to our smallness.

GILLIAN ALLNUTT

the displaced child

as if belonging were imaginable element

and she inhabitant

and she a star

in ether

rather

as her mother's industrial sewing-machine once requisitioned
    for—

worsted she said whatever

as if she'd been there—

in Łódź she meant for the whole of the war—

and now there were neither lodgement nor entitlement for her

*Łódź is known as 'the Polish Manchester'. Its textile industry was kept
going through World War II. Its Jewish cemetery is the largest in Europe.*

DAVID ATTWOOLL

Freedom from Torture

bread, n. (Old English) bit, piece, morsel

hljeb   dabo   khubz

related to *breowan*, brew, perhaps because
of the fermenting action of yeast, leavening

bara   borotho   mburu

once pronounced '*braid*' to rhyme with *break*
the old word *hlaf* survives in the modern *loaf*

ruti   canjeero   nan

Our baking group meets on Tuesday evenings
when the displaced and numb can speak

mkate   kikwanga   kobiz

and it helps to come and make simple things
kneading dough a haven, bread an innocent shore

panis   pita   pen

the smell of wholeness, home, before

CHRIS BECKETT

Earth's greeting to feet

Axee! I greet you, feet of the Afar and the Agaw

feet that cut salt-cakes out of my Great Depression
scribble up gullies and chutes

feet soft as bush-hares with fleshy ox-tongue toes
feet blackened by sunshine, soled with bauxite and copper

feet that madden flies with their otherworldly musk
tapping the slow-slow beat of dirges on my church forecourts

feet that cart whimper-babies and dizzy-dads out of my drought
    lands
that yoke a plough when the oxen are exhausted and my soil too
    tough

bare feet of Wollo and Tigray and Gojjam that are long and thin
    and gloriously leathered
that have never been shod and are their own shoes! their own
    shoe-laces!

feet dribbling a sockball, planting the crack of a whip
wading into my great pelican lakes riddled with bilharzia and
    cow-piss

feet that tick out marathons on the wooded slopes of Arsi
or scamper down hill-tracks to escape the shufti of the Ogaden
    (or any brigand looking for boots with an AK-47)

feet tripping towards the delirious shade of thorn bushes
    regardless of the risk of hyena or porcupine

and feet that leave their little bones in me, like Lucy, earliest
woman, light and pigeon-toed

feet that chatter about the past
feet that jump into the future

Lucy: in Amharic she is called Dinkenesh, meaning 'You are wonderful!'
She was found in the Afar region of north-east Ethiopia.

DENISE BENNETT

Making the Beds with Stanley Spencer

after Bedmaking by Stanley Spencer

We have wrapped the wounded
in warm quilts while
we struggle with hospital corners.
Stanley is shaking out
a wave of white cotton,
and I catch a glimpse of Christ
in his outstretched arms.

This is the last thing
we can do for them—a sacrament.
Nothing is more comforting
than the sweetness of clean sheets;
heads laid on soft pillows,
just below pin-ups of loved ones.
Even a priest couldn't match
the way we tuck them in.

STEVEN BLISS

Straniero

came unforeseen on a scrawny mare
from nowhere he would mention to stay
a couple of long months

carried gold in chunks not coins and a bag
of unpolished stones burning
fierce in the dark of his hands

was never messed with slept with wires
across his doorway a loaded gun
in hand and one by his pillow

and one day quietly saddled and left
the preacher gibbering the chapel ablaze
the school in riot and the marshal's wife
long barren now with child.

ALISON BRACKENBURY

Layout

Most houses had one, cold and small:
'front room'. Not 'lounge'. 'Parlour' was old,

though one great-aunt placed ferns on folds
of stacked cloths, stitched too fine to see.

I sometimes felt Victoria beamed.
sombrely on us. A 'settee'

too tall for father's mother's knees
filled ours, small table with a phone.

This, like our God, we left alone
in hope it might not notice us.

Dark cupboards, innocent of dust,
were burnished weekly, so the smell

of polish ruled. I could not tell
whether I loved or hated this

but lay there, by the fire's hiss,
held one evening. Then, a row:

the rosy candle melted down.
Like my grandparents, I have one

square room, where everything is done,
or not (for people eat on knees),

models are built on desks. Flowers please
my nose. Just sometimes, I recall

the tang of polish, and, for all,
another place, quite chill, and small.

CAROLE BROMLEY

On hearing for the first time

'It sounds very very high'

and she sobs for the joy of it,
for the reds and blues of it,
the shock, the hullabaloo,

the kerfuffle, the Sturm und Drang,
the sudden ice cream in a shake,
the sherbet firework burst.

'It's just amazing' she cries
her face in her hands.
'I'm going to say the months of the year'

and she hears them, shaking,
'January February March'
April overwhelms her.

It's like never having seen a bird,
or the sea or the stars
never tasting an orange,

like living all your life in a cave
and coming out into the light,
the sun on your face.

Afterwards she walks by the Tyne,
daren't go alone for fear
the birdsong, the traffic, the ship's hooter

will be too much. They are not.
It's like falling in love.

SARAH J. BRYSON

Teaching Verification of Death

Quiet is not what the ear expects
when the stethoscope is placed
over the chest, and to stop the sound
of the listener's own pulse
the trick is to let it go
let it just lie there.

As you listen, watch for any rise and fall
of breathing. Your eyes may deceive
when you do this, as their anticipation
of movement can override the truth
in the full minute which stretches out
through the silence of the darkened room.

Then lift each lid gently, shine
the penlight across, one at a time.
The pupils will be nonreactive, fixed,
and you'll know then what you knew
already and it's all right to cry,
only natural. I often do.

HANNE BUSCK-NIELSEN

A woman walks on the sea bed

a child clings to her back.
In one hand she carries a heavy suitcase,
in the other a small empty plastic bag.

The emptiness is full of footprints in mud,
little child-sized hands grasping for someone,
face after face—nobody she recognises.

One nobody is smiling—a bright flash.
She places a finger onto his lips' philtrum—
for a moment; his eyes shine so much.

It demands balance and co-ordination
to keep walking, to cross
through an ocean, its rush hour of the dead.

Her toenails' moons rise and wane
into the seabed. The child is silent.
The child eats shadow. Down here

the light gets darker. Darkness is a light
burden, when you carry emptiness
and nobody on the one hand,

and God knows what's in the suitcase.

OLIVIA BYARD

Muntjac Deer at Freeland

The despairing voice cries
'Kill the lot', as we hush
to watch a muntjac step lightly
onto the lawn, its curved back
a delicate question mark.
        'They gorge
themselves', the tart voice persists
as we're held by the sight
of this miracle of calm,
so close, so close.

(Of evolutionary interest
for their chromosome count,
descendants of escapes
from Woburn Abbey circa 1925,
these ancient orientals
have joined our herd and increased—
two have actually been seen near Belfast,
obviously with human help.)

'But so many make road-kill',
I demur, as the dainty deer
muzzles short clover and grass.
'Good,' comes the vengeful reply,
'they eat all my plants!'
        'Where
do they belong, who cares',
I wonder aloud, watching
tiny migrant hooves barely dent
the damp ground.

GILLIAN CLARKE

Daughter

i.m. April Jones 4/4/2007–1/10/2012

A pearl, April, born of water,
borne now in the river's arms,
child of the mountain,
mermaid of the estuary,
everyone's daughter.

Let her not be lost to the mothering sea.
Let her be light on the wave.
Let her change us forever.
Let us see her sweet face whenever
we gaze on the river, the sea,
like the moon on water.

Let this pain that is sleepless
lighten to love, to kindness.
Let ours be the arms that caught her,
love's weight, her light, the lightness
of everyone's daughter.

DAVID CONSTANTINE

The Marazion man

Waking I thought of the Marazion man
Who for the twelvemonth in all weathers
Took a camp chair to her grave and sat there
Telling her about his day. The long days were easiest
For then he need not visit till the promise of dusk
And perhaps by that time he had gone out with the starlings
To the North Coast and only set off home
To the South when they did. Those nights he slept.
He made sure to fix with her the hour of their conversation
And kept to it. He didn't want her worrying.
All the things were to say that had always been to say
And more, more, more that he could not bear she did not know
Till he told her. Hence his rush of words.
The short days were the worst. He thought it indecent
To haunt the common acre during the hours of darkness
And they were many and each one very long.
In daylight he was familiar, nobody accosted him.
He sat on his folding chair and told her his day
While the sun went down into the western sea.
Everyone in that place had a purpose
And how they managed was their own affair.
It is half a lifetime ago already.
The tombs have extended into the lower plots
Small decent necropolis growing in its own good time.
I shouldn't be able to find their stone among so many
But this morning I saw him alone out on the perimeter
Before there was a stone, while the earth was settling over her
And on his camp chair he was singular
Leaning forward, leaning down a little
Telling her his news, biding for hers.

DAVID COOKE

On My Daughter's Conversion to Islam

for Anna

How strange when I, who inherited faith
and kept it like a shabby gift, outgrown
and then abandoned, see how on your own
you have discovered a different path—

Islam, which, in the language you've studied
so well and love, I've learned has the meaning
surrender. You have seen light shining,
where I must shape my own less certain code.

Your daily prayers and recitation flow
serenely from the prophet's desert well,
a stream where each resonant syllable
is a pure sound whose music I'll allow,

noting again with pride the stubborn skill
you show in tracing its delicate script,
a calligraphy that's now implicit
in all you do, gracing the habitual.

And you showed courage, too, these troubled days
when you set yourself apart, your blazon
a scarf, which for some affronts their reason,
while extremists claim the airwaves.

It was not always so. Beneath the glare
of a Moorish sky I have looked to see
a formal garden, where geometry
and tempered light harmonize with water.

CLAIRE CROWTHER

Henge

for David Rogers

Mountain is made of stone. When stone breaks,
falls to be smoothed by the wash of sea and sand,
we can hold broken mountain in our hands.
Then we can build the mountain. Cairns of stones
mark our paths. At the end of a trail
the stone circle says *I have gone.*
Our circle is unfinished. Find a stone,
to make the rest endless with your own.

MARTYN CRUCEFIX

Resistance

after Laozi

Can you prevent your mind from straying—
can you hold to the one never let it slip

can you make your breath as soft as a child's
can you listen to its long-drawn out and in

can you renew the glass through which you gaze
so the world is whole and vivid

can you feel a love of others and persuade them
yet resist the desire to dictate

can you latch and unlatch the doors of perception
yet be content to play the female part

can your insight range and penetrate
far and near then back away do not interfere

then raise them every one—nourish them all
raise them but stake no claim

influence them but do not dictate
govern them but do not be drawn to legislate

only this my teacher says can be called power

SARAH DOYLE

Love Knots

Tie me a Rolling Hitch—
where a loose end is held
and takes a turn for the better;
where fibres grip hard,
never sliding apart.

Tie me a Sheet Bend—
where two ropes are coupled
and doubled for safety;
where difference is immaterial
if the bonds are true.

Tie me a Reef Knot—
where simplicity is everything
and transparency matters;
where strands clasp each other
in sinuous curves.

Tie me an Anchor Hitch—
where waters are dangerous
and horizons are changing;
where the line can take tension
but never wear thin.

Tie me a Blood Knot—
where substance is needed
and constancy called for;
where folds are drawn tightly,
withstanding all storms.

Tie me a Bowline—
where strength is important
and decades bear witness;
where shelter and refuge
are woven right through.

Tie me a Forget-Me-Knot—
where ends may be tattered,
but still coil together;
where impressions remain
when the knot is untied.

CLAIRE DYER

The Lamentations of Simultaneous Movements

Say I touch my face and in another world you touch yours.
What follows is a sort of keening.

> Somewhere a sun is glinting, the sky's cross-stitched
> with wind and wire and we are puppets.

Say I turn to face the water, there is wailing as you do the same.
Shadows rend the air,

> skim the ocean; the wash they leave behind is salty-blue.
> In both our places we are riven.

Say we learn to fly, soar high on thermals, hands cupped to our
    ears,
fugitives from separation.

> What follows will be hush, the banshees' surrender;
> their doeskin bags packed tight with raw laments.

CARRIE ETTER

Brazilian Birds

I luxuriate in subtitles, where language looks for a narrower passage, close to the bone as a cell. *Ornithologie brésilienne.* Gaze into rash colour. An eye surrounded by blue, then—yellow! Lemon-yellow feathers rising up, up in the smallest of Mohawks. *Histoire des oiseaux du Brésil.* Has a linguist catalogued the types of repetition? Reassertion, emphasis, disbelief. That long, long blue tail. What does it mean to look at birds? To watch otherness without assimilation? At last: *remarquable par leur plumage, leur chant.* Is enchantment enhanced by each sense added? Par leur plumage, leur chant, though the bright bright pages refuse to sing.

LAILA FARNES

After Afghanistan

Well into the indigo hour I drift
off, counting hundreds of doors.
I must be falling

grasp knobs, levers,
lock fingers onto a non-locking flare.
A portal opens

onto a blitz of West-Country
poppies
where a man stoops

to aim. Listen, ripe oranges
plummet, dragonflies
swarm. I hover

over snow-caps, gaping
mouths of sand,
turbans, babies turned

into cocoons, rows and rows.
I can't count
past the sum of many.

Sun's in my eyes,
the boom-slam of IEDs,
homes, bereft of doors.

VICKI FEAVER

The Stranger

Something made me look up
from my book—a consternation
in the crowd by the river,

as a man in pink trousers,
his legs the oxblood red
pink goes when it's wet,

dragged two children,
long wet hair straggling
over their faces, up the bank.

I was deep in a poem
when one child slipped
into a deep rocky cleft

in the river's shallow bed
and, panicking, pulled
her sister with her;

when the gurgling, gulping river
closed over their heads;
when a man walked out

of the woods and waded in
to save them—a stranger,
who as I ran to throw

my arms round my almost-
drowned daughters, strode
back into the trees.

SALLY GOLDSMITH

Are We There Yet?

Here—your hunched back chafes on a trolley
where you snatch each breath, exhale   *huh*

another, while two drunks bellow, set off an alarm
and I'm out on the low road, in for the ride, pretending calm

in this hell of a place you're dying in.   *Not long now*—
didn't you say that Mother, in your cherry dress, on our way

to Camber Sands, the suck and draw of waves?
I try to slow, to follow your shallow catch and   *huh*

until day is midnight and you're moved
to M.A.U. I moisten your lips and you mouth   *thank you*

to the nurse who is arranging your head.
Then morning, and loud round the bed, two doctors

too young to be doctors, crowd with their warming machine
and I slip between them and the uneasy chair which in any case

is too far back to see your mouth. Uncertain,
I drag a plastic one which scrapes just this side

of the curtain, across from the wheedling woman
and a raving one who refuses to give her fucking blood.

I look. Your mouth is cracked   *huh*
and I go out for a break. Just a breath of fresh air.

When I come back, it's late. You're already there.

25

CORA GREENHILL

Girls

The older women are always here
crouched on the beach over lumpy sacks,
pounding soaked coconut fibre on rocks
to soften it for rope. Though the boatmen
begin to use nylon now, the women,
wound in scarves, still labour like crabs
that dig endless holes in sand
to collapse with every tide.

But some schoolgirls from Makunduchi
came to the water this afternoon
still in their hijabs—
upright monochrome sea birds,
wading in the green prairie
of the shallow, outgoing tide.
Laughing, they stooped and scooped water,
splashed each other,
got the hems of their black skirts wet.

The girls stood out like a sign
among the rag bag of small boys
squealing in deep jade pools.
And three older boys, nonchalant
in football shirts, hovering,
swaggering, as boys do, held
in their sphere like Jupiter's moons,
circling but never touching.

We watched it all from a distance—
the girls being girls in the water
their white hijabs flapping: sails
straining in winds of change.

JOHN GREENING

A Letter to Mike Petrus

the voices of my accursed human education
D. H. Lawrence

I think I'd like to find two mountain lions in my back yard.
We've had a muntjac, our cat once brought a baby rabbit,
the usual selection of shrews and voles and mice—oh, and both
varieties of woodpecker, neither of them as striking
as that one with the magic fez who pattered on unfazed
while you were pointing out the winter quarters of a moth
defoliating your woods, those tents of caterpillar
in full battle gear. That was my exchange year, when the Gulf
was ablaze, Bush remaining unsinged. And the day we saw
a black bear, as if the myth had broken from a cocoon
of longing and even left its droppings for us there, warm
proof that if you wish on something that isn't Disney, it
can star for you in a lost silent picture, and unreel
beyond the Special Relationship, beyond D-Day and trench
tea-parties and all mad German kings . . . But your lions came
'to exchange long looks at twenty yards in the morning light'
and took up residence, you write, in a place unconsciously
made ready for them, beside the creek, where the mowing ends:
pumas, cougars, panthers, painters, catamounts, living
not anthologised with the dead and fabulous, nor preserved
by Frost's gaze in gladiatorial applause, but to make
themselves at home even as they stay apart, like old friends.

GABRIEL GRIFFIN

Blue and White China

In the square
a young boy
writes my name
on a grain of rice.
He's Chinese.

The Chinese
press grains of rice
into bone clay
before firing
blue and white china.

Blue and white china
held to the light reveals
rice shrouds, ghost grains,
names lost in the firing
in the square.

PHILIP GROSS

Thumbing,

bumming it, sleepwalking almost, down the hard shoulder,
Army Surplus parka on the droop of him,

this wan boy thinly dreadlocked
on the Penzance bypass, miles
from any lay-by, roundabout or turn,

he's fit to drop, one thumb hooked out at half mast,
hopeless, and the other in his mouth,

and past caring who sees it: shoppers out early
to Asda, late milk lorries, rattling delivery vans,
unseasonal tourists blown home by the spitting rain

or kids in tight surf buggy huddles, his age
but they won't stop, don't want to be touched

by whatever has touched him. Take me home,
the plugged-in thumb says, morning after
too much, too much, while the other drags him

on. Pull it out, he'd go down with a sigh;
there'd be crumpled fatigues, boots, nothing in them.

A. F. HARROLD

Nocturne: *California, February 26th 2007*

All day the sun whitened the world.
Its sharp fingers burnt where it brushed,
left shadows dark with draughtsman's edges.

Birds sang their chorus up until noon,
then left, off to sing elsewhere, perhaps,
or to find shade for their siestas.

I stayed in, half napped too.
I read books, noted the silence now and then.
Thought about you out in your lecture hall.

Now evening's rolling in.
I've switched the desk lamp on to write.
Through the slatted blinds the courtyard's dark,

but there I am, reflected in the glass,
scribbling away at this. How strange
to be in so many places at once:

here and there, for two;
in your mind for three; in mine for four.
And who can say where else?

Soon I'll switch off the light.

IAN HOUSE

The Last Meal

Last Meal on Death Row (photographs by Mat Collishaw)

Some chose the works: burritos, enchiladas,
tortillas, a cantaloup, whole, then split in half;

The world is iron   stone   unshaded lights.
Monastic.   A burrow.   A barracks.

Frank Garret ordered a chalice of colourful ice creams,
William Joseph Kitchens a stack of fried bread
and six eggs, sunnyside up, glimmering
against a night-black ground.

Our lives have been simplified.
You might call it a blessing.

You can imagine how James Russell's eyes
devoured his one perfect apple.

Time, wearisome as a concertina, stretches
and squeezes.

Six eggs, an apple: what in the end it came to,
the self's final assertion.

Choice is a wasted muscle.
Chance would be a fine thing.

WENDY KLEIN

The Sand Sweeper of Kovalam

She will not be eclipsed by the bedspread man,
who plays at statue-making; poses against
a seascape, a few palms for effect, his wares
perched on his head, fanned out in a pyramid
of rainbow pleats as he tempts passersby
with whirls of fabric. She just sweeps on,

decked out, in the violent chaos of colour
of roadside gardens where sudden poinsettias,
waggle their thick crimson tongues, spread
their flames against tea plantations,
green as envy that make a mockery
of English Christmases.

Where the rarer yellow-golds join in, cackle
at their scandal, I lose my bearings
as I try to imagine the sand sweeper at night;
where she goes, what she does in her spare time,
what exotic philosophy leads her to pick up
her renewable broom each day: if it is the grind

of guaranteed employment, its enforced ennui,
against the pedlar's hand-to-mouth challenge,
less predictable, more dramatic. I choose
to think of her with a belief in enchantment;
deep in the allure of taming the untameable,
of making sense of the vagrant sand.

GILL LEARNER

Was it for this

she'd carried the bulk of him, felt his kick
under her kanga, chewed her lip and thumped the wall
until he squawked in the hut's dim light?

She'd trekked to the well half an hour each way
with his sweet head nodding against her back
and empty-bellied had heaped his plate so he grew tall.

He'd walked three miles to the mission school
and learned to write and read and count
and vowed to build them a house one day.

They'd sold the camel to pay the man
who promised a bus, a boat, a job
in a glittering city across the sea.

She'd striped every sunset in soot on the wall
for a year and three days in withering hope.
Then the Aid man came to stammer his news

of a boat ablaze near a northern land.
A few had swum but many had drowned
and Kibwe, he feared, was one.

JENNY LEWIS

Non-military statements

1. Neutralization [*killing soldiers*] is part of any war
as are soft targets [*bombing civilians*].

2. Life deprivation [*killing anyone*] and surgical strikes
[*shelling and bombing*] can be justified.

3. Extraordinary rendition [*kidnapping*] of illegal combatants
[*people we don't like*] is necessary in the war against terror.

4. Enhanced coercive interrogation [*torture*] is used to get the
truth about weapons of mass destruction [*biological,
chemical, nuclear and imaginary*].

5. Collateral damage [*civilian deaths*] is unfortunate as is the
number of non-viable combat personnel [*wounded soldiers*].

6. The number of incidents of friendly fire [*accidentally killed by
own troops*] is regrettable as is the body count of non-operatives
[*dead soldiers*].

7. During war, more money can often be generated through
sales of weapons than in times of permanent pre-hostility
[peace].

PIPPA LITTLE

Against Hate

Sole passenger on an early morning tram
I'm half asleep when the driver brakes,
dashes past me, dives into a copse of trees,
gone for so long I almost get out to walk.
Then he's back, his face alight.
I saw the wren! Explaining
how he feeds her when he can
and her restless, secretive waiting.
We talk of things we love until the station.

I tell him of the Budapest to Moscow train
brought to a halt in the middle of nowhere,
everyone leaning out expecting calamity
but not the engine driver, an old man,
kneeling to gather armfuls of wild lilies,
wild orchids. He carried them back
as you would a newborn, top-heavy, gangly,
supporting the frail stems in his big, shovel hands.
These are small things, but I pass them on

because today is bloody, inexplicable
and this is my act, to write, feeling the light against my back.

KATHLEEN McPHILEMY

Blue Girl

for Rebecca and her parents

Blue girl
dancing on the rim of darkness,
your spangled blue dress
the empty promise of stars.

Your eye-shadow forecast your weather:
purple was challenging, stormy;
green was sullen, morose
while blue was hyper and happy
skittering across the campus
and the glitter as always was change.

The wood was polished and golden,
light streamed in from the window,
and your coffin also was light,
bright, covered with flowers.

Here is the trick of appearance,
darkness is locked inside;
eyes just closed for a moment,
and you sank through the well-oiled doors.

You peeled back the skin of the earth
to a red that is closer to black,
you robbed everyday of its colours
of its softness, hardness and roundness,
its changes of leaves and of water,
its solidity of doors and of trees.
Our days are as thin as paper,
our nights cling wrap the darkness.

Blue girl—
you danced too close to the edge,
trying to keep your balance
right at the rim of the world.

MARTIN MALONE

Let Us Sleep Now

Vienna, 31/7/2014

Then you spot him after all these years,
on the U3 platform at the *Westbahnhof*
heading out towards Simmering.

You glimpse his profile in the tunnel's gloom
but can't quite root that lean face,
clean and good-looking and well again.

The long summer heatwave's been good to him,
tanning his skin caramel and free
of the pallor of your last strange meeting.

A tattooed bicep strains impressively
at the t-shirt, a booted calf flexes
and there he stands in his animal prime.

You smile with recognition, catch his eye;
not Saxon or Prussian or Pomeranian
just an Austrian boy heading west again,
not your way but up the line to Simmering.

SIMON MARTIN

Where two rivers meet

Late August, cool wind, and sun, the cusp
of summer and autumn, heading on up
through banked and dappled lanes, workday calm,
to Wicklow's familiar hills when we heard

on the car radio. Useless to think
we'd stop and take it in more thoroughly
but stop we did, in a shaded passing place
in a hollow where two rivers meet.

And there, out in the current—fly fishers
in full sunlight, thigh deep, green-girdled, braced
to take the flow, tying their hooked lures tight
with rough, agile hands, then sending them out

in pulsing weighted arcs. Deft flicks of wrist
mended and trimmed, the water's whorled surface
gliding on through, as they waited for a stir,
ready to answer the deep-tugged tautness.

And I thought of you, out in the lit stream,
confluent, quietly broaching Moore's waters
working the reel, flicking and looping again,
showing us all how to cast the line.

Seamus Heaney died on 30 August 2013.

KATRINA NAOMI

The Woman who Married the Berlin Wall

fell in love at the age of seven, thrilling

to this Berliner's slim sensuality,
his horizontal lines, his sense of division;
found the Great Wall of China *far too stout.*

She used the words *he* or *my husband,*
made models of her lover, took him on sleigh rides
so he could enjoy her native northern Sweden.

She papered her rooms from bulging scrapbooks.
On her sixth visit, they wed: a small ceremony.
She scratched her desire deep into his core;
knowing he couldn't leave until he was demolished,
chunk by chunk. She felt she owned him outright.

I have some sympathy for a woman who could love a wall.
I have practised kissing tables, licking car seats,
have pressed myself against an aeroplane's wing.

CHRISTOPHER NORTH

AK47

You don't see these much
in the to-ing and fro-ing of our village.

People would recognize them
from the TV. Men would be easy

with the idea of them, small boys too
but there's no general aspiration to own one,

not in this settled, daily, dull
baker, fishmonger, corner bar

little cluster of routines and lotteries
that is our village in a peaceful country.

Though who knows what is brewing
behind those expressionless doors?

Who knows what is in the mind
of the youth in the bus shelter, foot juddering?

The morning is quiet. People are walking
towards the market. The day is drunk

with normality so this artefact
is far from people's minds;

would be as strange as a naked woman
cradling a water-melon as if it was a baby

or the old men sitting on the wall
suddenly rising smartly to attention.

41

NIGEL PANTLING

The Bulb Fields

Heads are down, backs are bent,
legs are splayed, knees are braced,
right hands break the fossil crust
(routing stones with whittled nails)

left hands clutch the scaly bulbs,
dropping one in every pit,
then the backfill, press the clay,
slouch ten inches up the row.

In the break, they have time only
to nod, smoke, swallow coffee,
exchange names: tulipano,
tulpe, tiúilipí, tulppaani, tulp,

before the drizzle drives them back—
dig, plant, cover, shuffle on
dig, plant, cover, shuffle on
—towards their quota for the day.

ANNA ROBINSON

Agnus

Lamb, I have seen you from trains.
I have seen you as I walked through fields.
You looked back at me, raised
your left hoof towards me in a delicate way.
Lamb, I have found your winter curls
by the roadside, on thorns and on barbed wire.

Lamb, who exalts what the world gets wrong
its failings, its struggles, honourable lamb
feel for us.

Lamb, all winter I wear black to absorb the sun.
Red is not as good at this. It is only for inside.
Lamb, my mother had a dream.
The whole family lived separately in sheds
in the back yard. It was dark and cold.
When we went to find each other, we weren't there.

Lamb, who exalts what the world gets wrong
heals wounds, smooths troubles, loving lamb
feel for us.

Lamb, these derelict testaments are stained.
They're cased in walls of clay. We cannot reach them.
We are damp and raucous, our marsh overgrown.
The trees under our pavements are dead. The stairs,
by which you left to sail up river, lead nowhere.
Lamb, why do we fear ourselves?

Lamb, who exalts what the world gets wrong
crowns hags, creates doubt, fragrant lamb
give us peace.

PETER ROBINSON

A Period Sky

1

Today the sky has a period flavour,
distances whipped in by cumulus piles
covering ranges of blue
from a near turquoise through to deep azure.
Anachronistic vapour trails
intersperse grey-bellied cloud-heaps;
they rise above chimney brick, half-timbered gable,
a pink tinge on every ply.

2

Enough to make weak eyes water, the sky
bares a memory of pain
to which your heart goes out . . .
Sharp on the tongue, and getting keener,
it's tickled by a kitchen garden's
fennel, thyme, rosemary, lemon verbena.

3

As if we could still hear the shrieks and far cries
worked by a Topcliffe or Ketch,
I'm wincing at the thought of it,
that torture, while gone on above it,
clouds in all their gory detail,
their glory continue to trail
at dusk . . . oh empty, indifferent sky!

ELISABETH ROWE

Shadow Selves

They are there in the dark of us,
shackled and dungeoned
out of mind.

We pass them cups of water,
scraps of bread,
curious to look into their eyes
and see our own violence
shining there.

Sometimes when we need the spice
of power or pain
we let them out;

mostly we shut them up
like the Inuit woman
who went about all winter

gathering shadows into boxes
so that when spring came
there would be light.

ANNA SAUNDERS

Played

Pan has watched Syrinx glide underwater,
pale and luminous as a drowned moon.

Now crouched on the bank, he paws her out.
Water bangles the nymphs' wrists as they reach for her.

Only briefly is she that pale reed, wavering,
as dragon flies dart emerald needles into the bank.

He will whittle her stem with steel, hack at her
until only a stump remains
take her other half, cold and empty, to his lips.

He will use her to bring Diana down from the sky,
blow his song through her echo chamber,
her emptiness amplifying his calls.

MYRA SCHNEIDER

Women Running

after Picasso: Deux femmes courant sur la plage

Look how their large bodies leaping
from dresses fill the beach, how their breasts
swing happiness, how the mediterraneans
of sea and sky fondle their flesh. Nothing

could rein them in. The blown wildnesses
of their dark animal hair, their hands joined
and raised, shout triumph. All their senses
are roused as they hurtle towards tomorrow.

That arm laid across the horizon,
the racing legs, an unstoppable quartet, pull
me from my skin and I become one of them,
believe I'm agile enough to run a mile,

believe I'm young again, believe age
has been stamped out. No wonder, I worship
at the altar of energy, not the energy huge
with hate which revels in tearing apart,

in crushing to dust but the momentum
which carries blood to the brain, these women
across the plage, lovers as they couple,
and tugs at the future till it breaks into bloom.

PENELOPE SHUTTLE

Heart?

When I perform a miracle
    Heart yawns.

Heart never tried to be good
    or mend its ways.

Heart can carry its own weight
    in gold or despair or wickedness for miles.

These days Heart never asks for teddy
    to be tucked up alongside Heart at bedtime.

Heart hammers
    on the bloodstone of my ear,

the sorrow-sound gets bigger,
    yelling me to pieces. Result.

Heart skedaddles away
    on its next dreadful mission.

HYLDA SIMS

The Temporary Lodger

You've gone back now, no permit here for you.
There used to be an email time to time, but now
I don't know where or how or if you are.
We were never lovers—friends, that's all.

I never felt the scars that laced your back
or understood what screamed inside your head
when you went silent; you'd talk of home but not
of those bad days—you never spoke of that.

Sometimes you seemed so private, wouldn't eat—
I'd hear you walking round the house at night.
I wish I'd asked you, made you open up—
maybe I couldn't face such pain—instead

I taught you how to swear in English, bake
an apple crumble; you repaired the legs
on my old kitchen chairs, we'd walk till dark
in Sydenham Woods or over Brockwell Park

then stroll back home for tea; the wars went on
all summer, lies and limbs and bodybags—
Afghanistan, Iraq, and Lebanon—
we watched it on the telly; now you've gone

the wars have not, but still you fill my head.
I've left the world to nincompoops and thugs.
It's hard to grieve for half a million dead
but then there's you, oh, I miss you, my friend . . .

ANDREW SMARDON

Roman site 42, Turkey

They had told us about the buried town,
but not the drowning village. Both unnamed
on all our current maps, although this place
is a confluence of dialects and tongues.

Inside our fence, we dig, then re-cover
the Roman halls and markets. Outside
soldiers flood the living streets, hauling off
zinc roofs and bulldozing cinderblock walls.

In six weeks they will cap out the dam
and anything we cannot lift or log
will drown. One town we will bury to save.
The other will never have been here.

ANNE STEWART

Very Hard Indeed?

What do I know of such things?
Only what you feel when truth of it cannot be denied.
Only the roiling acid down deep inside?
And the wish that blinds your eyes.

How can we do such things?
A marriage of skills and circumstance
to fear and fear of ignorance . . .
But you already know this.

How can we heal such things?
How can we make it right?
Oh, but, never truly. How could you think otherwise?
For your guilt, you might apologise . . .

How can we put stop to such things?
Die. All die.
But won't we change in time? Lose our talent for barbarity?
Hmm. Some progress has been made . . .

How much harder are you willing to try?

GILLIAN STONEHAM

Watching Sheep

A five-barred gate and a person looking
and listening
to the soft velcro tearing of grass,
the busy grasping of each new mouthful,
all to be digested later
at undisturbed leisure.

Now and then a sheep will pause
to rub a flank and leave
her wispy signature curling on comfort of wood;
returning then to the separation of grass
that fills the field
and mingles with a floating smell of may
and the downward flight of petals
from spikes of chestnut's bursting pyramids.

From time to time another ewe
will raise her head as if to weigh up
whether a person leaning on a gate
is important enough to stare at
or possibly
not.

JUDI SUTHERLAND

Wanderer

for Fabrice Muamba

It's always been a game with heart-stopping
moments, but we didn't expect that invisible tackle,
that sudden foul that took you out of play;
your athlete's body, stumbled to a stop,
ashing on the touchline to a cooling grey
the crowd, hands over mouths, watching you drop
while the TV cameras decorously panned away.

Did your soul go flying, like a skied free kick,
up above the green bowl of White Hart Lane,
flipping over like a tossed coin: *heads tails heads?*
Did you see the coaches and the physios run on
applying the defibrillator? Did you know you were dead,
watching the hi-vis huddle of medics
unable to join the halves of you together again?

Did you find yourself pushing at a heavy door
that led to a dim, steamy dressing room
where Matt Busby, Stanley Matthews, Georgie Best
asked you how the fuck you'd got yourself sent off so soon?
Were there other voices echoing, guys getting dressed
after showers, packing kit bags, heading home?
Seventy-eight minutes. A team talk, a short rest

then did your studs clatter down the players' tunnel once more
to the bright floodlit glory of Saturday afternoon?

*Bolton Wanderers footballer Fabrice Muamba suffered a cardiac arrest
while playing against Spurs in March 2012. His heart stopped for over an
hour before he was revived.*

MICHAEL SWAN

Sardanes

I should like the world to end
in just this way.

Eight musicians
in the town square.

People arrive
a few at a time
join hands
and begin dancing.

Four steps to the left
four to the right.
Hands held high
in a flower pattern.

Little by little
more come
to join the circles
and dance gravely

until at the end
with hands held high
in a flower pattern
the whole world dances

to eight musicians
in the town square.

Sardanes are traditional Catalan folk dances.

SUSAN UTTING

Night Apples

And she woke to the trees all bare,
the fruit gone from them, as if
a thief had shaken them down
to a blanket spread on the ground,
the rough, root-swallowed ground.

As if they'd been scooped up,
made fast in a woven wool cloth,
four corners knotted and pinned,
slung over a shoulder, the back
blades of a giant, a light-fingered

Atlas, who'd carried them off
in the soft nap of night, under
the cover of this, heat-laden night,
to be scattered, tipped at the feet
of an object of love; to be tasted,

sweet as the kiss of a stranger,
a true kiss, not stolen but gathered.

KATE VENABLES

Reconstruction

The wound's not the thing, it's the trust—
young faces with clear eyes looking straight
at you above slipped jaws, open mouths,
loose tongue, swollen lips. Survivors, hopeful—
you can almost feel the soft curls
of beard on cheeks and neck—
back in Blighty for a good long stay
out of it for good and this man Gillies
is good they say. I'll wait a bit then get
the nurse to write my girl.
It's the 'after' faces
above their jackets and ties
that are wary, guarded, scapegoated,
lonely. Not seen, not recognised.

Henry Tonks was a surgeon and artist who worked with Harold Gillies,
the pioneer facial surgeon. The Royal College of Surgeons holds a collection
of his pastels of the faces of men wounded in the First World War, before
and after reconstructive surgery.
http://www.gilliesarchives.org.uk/Tonks%20pastels/index.html

CHRISTINE WEBB

Cocklers

Half dusk. Low water. A frieze
of figures stooping, ankle-deep, dark
on dark, in a slow tide they might have crawled from,
scaly feet and fingers gripping rock.

But these are men, living on the hard tack
of hope, wrenching the tough salt of their wages
—a sea traffic so hidden, for all we know
scrimshaws record its tools and practices.

Methodical as potato-pickers, they bend,
sweep, gather, stow, ignoring the web
of cold that gathers between fingers and toes
and the white combs of the waves rolling up

to drown the ribbed tracks to safety. Already
men flounder in the long swell, gulping
the tide until it swallows them, mouths
open in silent Os, bodies turning

cartwheels in the undertow, pulled further
and further on the current's thread, flotsam
that drifts, tumbles, finds the shore too late—
known by a single tooth or a lucky charm.

SUSAN WICKS

This Art

Museum of Inuit Art, Toronto

This art tells stories of a few known things
in black and white, of seals and walruses and bears
and caribou in ivory or rock; the close dark hives
of igloos; fish. A soapstone woman kneels,
her two white plaits escaping from her hood.

Here are the huntings and migrations,
kayaks and dog-teams and pack-sledges
Carved out of stone or horn, and polished smooth
as if by ice. Here is the owl-man waiting, here's the wife
stretching her skins, the otter suckling, the two bears in rut.

The Inuit mother in her dark *aumak*
is a girl with two heads: her new-born child
grows from her shoulders. Everything she sees
her child sees too, each tiny carving cries
its uses. Every toothpick is a small harpoon.

Two seated figures hold their arms outstretched
from their muffled trunks, as if each contact hurts.
The cribbage boards are little ivory boats
with bears for figureheads, their intricate pale decks
pierced by ten dozen holes.

MARGARET WILMOT

Self-Portraits

The kid in the train is noisy, abuses the young man
selling beer. *Aren't you a Moslem, man?*
Would you charge me that if I was starving?
He's making his way, he tells us, from Parkhurst
back to Clapham. *Three years since I been out,*
got six but I was enhanced. He sounds scared.
But now I got it in me. Convincing himself.
Before, you could see through me, nothing there.
When we get out, he shakes our hands, can't stop thanking us.
I wish I'd said *Don't hassle Hindus, for a start.*
At the exhibition Joshua Reynolds screens his eyes
behind a bar of shadow; it's his openness which draws me in,
face looking through itself and out into the scary world.
Later I pass a poster for *The 400 Blows*: we know
this boy who's peering through the wire fence.

ANTHONY WILSON

Three Pieces (Poem Beginning with a Line by Yehuda Amichai)

The rain is my home.
It wraps its arms around me
whispering words of hope.
The rain is falling.
It greets me with a kiss.
Three times it kisses me,
a mother sending her child
to be good at school.
The rain is kind,
it knows my name,
it is not cold.
It buys me a new coat,
it stays to water my garden.
The rain comes to me
as a memory of one boy
punching another,
but this soon ceases.
The rain promises
it will never leave.
It leaves me
by the river, into which it flows.
There are ducks there
and children throwing bread
shouting 'Ducks!'

*

I walk in the rain.
It is raining,
my head is wet,
my unprotected head

61

my only protection.
I am happy to be
in the rain, happy
as it slides
from my face.

*

I have become the rain.
Its bones are mine,
supple and soft
in the wind.
I turn this way and that
among its fine rods,
I do not deserve it.
I have no shadow.
I long to become one
with the rain.
I do not understand
who the rain wants me to be.
It takes my hand,
I follow, saying yes.
The rain is in my arms,
I am in the arms of the rain.
I walk in its wandering voice,
far from myself,
I am home.

PAT WINSLOW

Beyond Frame

for Talha

The prisoner steps into the painting his brother made for him.
He knows there's no going back, that he must learn to swim

through colour, trust negative space, seek a vanishing line.
In time, he may decide that the cell he is leaving behind

is a cube and cubes can be undone and spread out, made flat
like a net diagram. Walking in blue and orange he'll find that

parallel lines often meet, that sound travels best by pen and ink.
Nothing is more profound than the silence of green, he'll think.

And though he might not see his brother, he will on occasion
hear him sing. He'll recognise the familiar scent of his skin

which is not unlike his own. Today, stepping out into the light,
he is stripped clean. He is his brother's breath, without weight.

Nothing can detain him. He is beyond the margins of time,
beyond anything that suggests containment, beyond frame.

DOROTHY YAMAMOTO

My father remembers Aijiro's horse

There were many horses in the village
but only one beautiful one.
It belonged to Aijiro, the cavalry officer,
who groomed it lovingly, never worked it hard,
fretted when it stepped on ice.

Every summer there were races
at Takamiya, along a dried-up river bed.
All the farm horses in the neighbourhood—
fat, thin, tall, short—
clopped along to take part.
The farmers' boys strapped cushions on their backs
but the horses, who were used to pulling carts,
bucked and whinnied madly.

At the finishing line an official
dangled pieces of paper—
first, second, third—to be grabbed by the jockeys
as they stampeded past.
First prize was, say, a bamboo rake
or a wooden tub or bucket
with money in it—five yen, perhaps.

Aijiro never entered his horse for the race
although, my father said,
half understanding, half not,
it would have won, easily.

About the Poets

Afam Akeh is a significant voice in contemporary Nigerian poetry, and has work in two published volumes of poetry and some anthologies. In recent years he has been involved with literature development work, with a particular interest in African writing.

Gillian Allnutt was writer in residence with Freedom from Torture/The Medical Foundation in North-East England in 2009-10.

David Attwooll's poems have appeared in various magazines, anthologies, and two pamphlets (*Surfacing* and *Ground Work*), and his collection *The Sound Ladder* (Two Rivers Press) was published in April 2015.

Chris Beckett grew up in Ethiopia in the days of Haile Selassie. His collection *Ethiopia Boy* was published by Oxford Poets/Carcanet in 2013.

Denise Bennett has an MA in creative writing and runs poetry workshops in community settings. Her work has been widely published and she has two collections, *Planting the Snow Queen* and *Parachute Silk*, both published by Oversteps Books.

Steven Bliss grew up in Sheffield, read English at Cambridge and now lives near Oxford. He started to write poems seven years ago: a few have been published in magazines and anthologies.

Alison Brackenbury's most recent collection of poems (her eighth) is *Then*, published by Carcanet in 2013.

Carole Bromley has a first collection, *A Guided Tour of the Ice House,* with Smith/Doorstop and a second book, *The Stonegate Devil,* coming out in October 2015.

Sarah J. Bryson writes poems and short stories. She takes photos nearly every day and works as a hospice nurse, part-time. Her work has been placed in competitions and published in various forms: in anthologies, in journals, and online.

Hanne Busck-Nielsen is Danish, born in Copenhagen, and came to the UK to study psychology and psychoanalysis. Her poems have appeared in various anthologies and her translations of one of Denmark's major contemporary poets, Henrik Nordbrandt, were published in *POEM, International English Language Journal.*

Olivia Byard's third collection, *The Wilding Eye: New and Selected Poems,* published in April 2015, was made a *New Statesman* recommended read in June 2015. A recording of a previous reading she gave in Oxford in aid of Freedom from Torture can be heard on her website: www.oliviabyard.com

Gillian Clarke is the National Poet of Wales, and the President of Ty Newydd, the writers' centre in North Wales which she co-founded in 1990. Her latest collection is *Ice* (Carcanet, 2012).

David Constantine's most recent collection of poems is *Elder* (Bloodaxe, 2014).

David Cooke has been widely published in the UK, Ireland, and beyond. His most recent collection, *Work Horses* (Ward Wood Publishing), came out in 2012, and his next, *A Murmuration,* will be published by Two Rivers Press in 2015.

Claire Crowther has published three collections of poems, including her latest, *On Narrowness* (Shearsman, 2015), and four pamphlets.

Martyn Crucefix's recent original collections include *Hurt* (Enitharmon, 2010), *The Time We Turned* (Shearsman, 2014), *A Hatfield Mass* (Worple Press, 2014). He has translated Rilke's *Duino Elegies* (Enitharmon, 2006)—shortlisted for the 2007 Popescu Prize for European Poetry Translation—and Rilke's *Sonnets to Orpheus* (Enitharmon, 2012). *Daodejing—a new version in English* will be published in 2016. For more visit www.martyncrucefix.com

Sarah Doyle is Poet-in-Residence to the Pre-Raphaelite Society. Her poems have been widely placed and published, and PS Publishing brought out her first collection, *Dreaming Spheres: Poems of the Solar System* (co-written with Allen Ashley), in 2014. Sarah reads frequently at poetry events, and co-hosts *Rhyme & Rhythm Jazz-Poetry Club* at the Dugdale Theatre, Enfield.

Claire Dyer's poetry collection, *Eleven Rooms*, is published by Two Rivers Press. Her novels, *The Moment* and *The Perfect Affair*, and her short story, *Falling for Gatsby*, are published by Quercus. She has an MA in Creative Writing from Royal Holloway, University of London.

Carrie Etter's most recent collection, *Imagined Sons* (Seren, 2014), was shortlisted for the Ted Hughes Award for New Work in Poetry by The Poetry Society. She has taught creative writing at Bath Spa University since 2004.

Laila Farnes was born in Somalia and raised in Port-of-Spain, Trinidad and Tobago. She now lives in Norway. Laila completed an MA in Creative Writing at Lancaster in 2008.

Vicki Feaver lives in Scotland on the edge of the Pentland Hills. The poems in her last two collections, *The Handless Maiden* (Cape, 1994) and *The Book of Blood* (Cape, 2006), often combine fairytale or myth with contemporary experience. She is currently completing a collection focusing on childhood and old age.

Sally Goldsmith lives in Sheffield and is a writer of poems, songs, and verse drama.

Cora Greenhill's poetry often illuminates those moments when people of different cultures suddenly connect and we see each other and the world in a new way. Her latest book, *The Point of Waking* (Oversteps, 2013), contains many poems set in Crete and others from travels in Africa.

John Greening's most recent books are *To the War Poets* (Oxford Poets/Carcanet, 2013), *Accompanied Voices: Poets on Composers from Thomas Tallis to Arvo Pärt* (Boydell, 2015), and a new edition of Edmund Blunden's *Undertones of War* (OUP, 2015).

Gabriel Griffin, poet and author, is the creator of Poetry on the Lake international events.

Philip Gross is the author of eighteen collections of poetry since 1983; the latest is *Love Songs of Carbon* (Bloodaxe, 2015).

A. F. Harrold is an English poet and performer who writes for adults and children. Much of his poetry is published by Two Rivers Press and his children's fiction by Bloomsbury. www.afharrold.com.

Ian House taught in England, Eastern Europe, and the United States. His collections are *Cutting the Quick* (2005) and *Nothing's Lost* (2014), both with Two Rivers Press.

Wendy Klein, a retired psychotherapist, is published in many magazines and anthologies. Winner of the Cinnamon Press Single Poem Competition 2014, she has two collections from Cinnamon: *Cuba in the Blood* (2009) and *Anything in Turquoise* (2013) with a third in progress.

Gill Learner has been widely published, won a few competitions, has one collection, *The Agister's Experiment* (Two Rivers Press, 2011), and hopes to have another in 2016.

Jenny Lewis is a poet and playwright. Her recent work includes *Taking Mesopotamia* (Oxford Poets/Carcanet, 2014) and *Singing for Inanna*, poems in English and Arabic with the Iraqi poet Adnan al-Sayegh (Mulfran Press, 2014). She teaches poetry at Oxford University.

Pippa Little is a poet who lives in Northumberland. She is a Royal Literary Fund Fellow at Newcastle University. Her collection, *Overwintering*, is published by Carcanet (2012).

Kathleen McPhilemy was born in Belfast but lives in Oxford. She has published three collections, the most recent being *The Lion in the Forest* (Katabasis, 2004).

Martin Malone was born in County Durham and now lives in Scotland. He has published two poetry collections: *The Waiting Hillside* (Templar, 2011) and *Cur* (Shoestring, 2015). An Honorary Research Fellow in Creative Writing at Aberdeen University, he is currently studying for a PhD at Sheffield University. He edits *The Interpreter's House* poetry journal.

Simon Martin read German and English Literature at The Queen's College, Oxford, and now lives in Oxford and Berlin with his young family.

Katrina Naomi's latest collection, *The Way the Crocodile Taught Me*, will be published by Seren in 2016. www.katrinanaomi.co.uk

Christopher North facilitates residential poetry courses at Almassera Vella in Alicante, Spain. He has published four collections, the most recent *Wolves Recently Sighted* (Templar Poetry, 2014).

Nigel Pantling lives in North London. His first collection, *Belfast Finds Log*, was published by Shoestring Press in 2014.

Anna Robinson was born and lives in London. Her publications include *The Finders of London* (Enitharmon, 2010) and *Into the Woods* (Enitharmon, 2014).

Peter Robinson has published many volumes of poetry and translations, for some of which he has received the Cheltenham Prize, the John Florio Prize, and two Poetry Book Society Recommendations. Recent publications include *Foreigners, Drunks and Babies: Eleven Stories* (Two Rivers Press, 2013), a collection of poems called *Buried Music* (Shearsman Books, 2015), and one of prose poems and memoirs, *The Draft Will* (Isobar Press, 2015).

Elisabeth Rowe lives on Dartmoor, writes both serious and comic poetry, and has three collections published: *Surface Tension* (Peterloo Poets, 2003), *Thin Ice* (Oversteps Books, 2010), and *Taking Shape* (Oversteps Books, 2013).

Anna Saunders is the author of *Communion* (Wild Conversations Press, 2011), *Struck* (Pindrop Press, 2014), and *Kissing the She Bear* (Wild Conversations Press, 2015). She has had poems published in journals and anthologies, including *Ambit, The North, Amaryllis, Iota, Caduceus, Envoi, The Wenlock Anthology 2014,* and *The Museum of Light.*

Myra Schneider has published several collections of poetry, most recently *The Door to Colour* (Enitharmon, 2014) and her other publications include books about personal writing.

Penelope Shuttle lives in Cornwall. Her pamphlet *In the Snowy Air* appeared from Templar in 2014. Her eleventh full collection, *Will You Walk A Little Faster*, appears from Bloodaxe on Shuttle's 70th birthday in May 2017.

Hylda Sims's poetry is published by Hearing Eye Books. She writes poems, songs, and novels and runs a monthly poetry and music event, Fourth Friday, at the Poetry Café, Covent Garden, London.

Andrew Smardon lives in Oxfordshire with his wife. He is active in a number of workshops in Oxford and London, including Tideway Poets, and his work has been published in *Stand*, *Iota*, and *Oxford Magazine*.

Anne Stewart runs the poet showcase, www.poetrypf.co.uk and is the Administrator for Second Light, a network of women poets. She won the Bridport Prize in 2008 and her collection, *The Janus Hour*, is published by Oversteps Books (2010).

Gillian Stoneham's *When That April* (1960) was published by Chatto & Windus with the Hogarth Press in their Phoenix Living Poets series. Since then many of her poems have appeared in magazines.

Judi Sutherland works in Biotechnology and lives in Barnard Castle, Durham. Her poems have been widely published in magazines and online, including *Acumen*, *New Statesman*, *And Other Poems*, and *Ink, Sweat and Tears*. She blogs at www.judisutherland.com and is the editor of poetry webzine *The Stare's Nest*.

Michael Swan works in applied linguistics, and writes poetry in a desperate attempt to prove that grammarians have souls.

Susan Utting's poems have been widely published including in *The Times, TLS, The Independent, Forward Book of Poetry, The Poetry Review,* and *Poems on the Underground.* Following *Striptease* (Smith/Doorstop) and *Houses Without Walls* (Two Rivers Press), *Fair's Fair* (also Two Rivers Press, 2012) is her latest poetry collection.

Kate Venables is a physician and also a student in the creative writing programme at the University of Oxford. Her work has appeared in various magazines, including *Ink, Sweat and Tears, Envoi, Brittle Star,* and *Lighthouse.*

Christine Webb's *After Babel* was published in 2004 by Peterloo; *Catching Your Breath* (Cinnamon Press, 2011) celebrates and mourns her partner of 40 years. Her work has appeared in a range of magazines and anthologies.

Susan Wicks's seventh collection, *The Months,* will be published by Bloodaxe in 2016. Her second book-length translation of the French poet Valerie Rouzeau, *Talking Vrouz,* won the Oxford-Weidenfeld Prize in 2014.

Margaret Wilmot was born in California, and worked in the Mediterranean and New York before moving to Sussex in 1978. Her pamphlet, *Sweet Coffee* (2013), is published by Smiths Knoll.

Anthony Wilson's latest book is *Lifesaving Poems* (Bloodaxe, 2015). He lives and works in Exeter.

Pat Winslow's seventh collection, *Kissing Bones,* is published by Templar Poetry. For further information visit www.patwinslow.com

Dorothy Yamamoto lives in Oxford, where she helps to run poetry group Oxford Stanza 2. Many of her poems explore her Japanese heritage. Her collection, *Landscape with a Hundred Bridges*, is published by Blinking Eye.

Acknowledgements

David Attwooll, 'Freedom from Torture' is reprinted from *The Sound Ladder* (Two Rivers Press, 2015) with grateful acknowledgements to the publisher.

Carole Bromley, 'On hearing for the first time' appears in the 2015 Hippocrates Prize Anthology.

Olivia Byard, 'Muntjac Deer at Freeland' was first published in *Quadrant* (Australia).

Carrie Etter, 'Brazilian Birds' was first published in *Poetry Wales*.

Sally Goldsmith's 'Are We There Yet?' is the title poem of her collection published by Smith/Doorstop in 2013.

Cora Greenhill, 'Girls' was first published in *Artemis*.

A. F. Harrold, 'Nocturne: *California, February 26th 2007*' was first published in *Of Birds & Bees* (Quirkstandard's Alternative, 2008).

Gill Learner, 'Was it for this' was first published in the Spring 2014 edition of *Poetry News*.

Jenny Lewis, 'Non-Military Statements' is reprinted from *Taking Mesopotamia* (Oxford Poets/Carcanet, 2014), by kind permission of the publisher.

Pippa Little, 'Against Hate' first appeared in the online poetry magazine *The Compass*.

Martin Malone, 'Let Us Sleep Now' was first published in *Agenda*.

Simon Martin, 'Where two rivers meet' was first published in *The North*.

Katrina Naomi, 'The Woman Who Married the Berlin Wall' was first published in the Scottish/US poetry magazine *The Dark Horse*.

Nigel Pantling, 'The Bulb Fields' was first published in *Magma*.

Anna Robinson, 'Agnus', is reprinted from *The Finders of London* (Enitharmon, 2010), by kind permission of the publisher.

Peter Robinson, 'A Period Sky' is reprinted from *The Returning Sky* (Shearsman, 2012), by kind permission of the publisher.

Elisabeth Rowe, 'Shadow Selves' is reprinted from *Thin Ice* (Oversteps Books, 2010), by kind permission of the publisher.

Anna Saunders, 'Played', is reprinted from *Kissing the She Bear* (Wild Conversations Press, 2015).

Myra Schneider, 'Women Running' is reprinted from *What Women Want* (Second Light Publications, 2012).

Michael Swan, 'Sardanes' appears in the Ver Poets Competition Anthology.

Kate Venables, 'Reconstruction' was first published in *Ink, Sweat and Tears*.

Christine Webb, 'Cocklers' was first published in *Catching Your Breath* (Cinnamon Press, 2011).

Margaret Wilmot, 'Self-Portraits' was first published in *Staple*.

Anthony Wilson, 'Three Pieces (Poem Beginning with a Line by Yehuda Amichai)' was first published in *The North*.

Dorothy Yamamoto, 'My father remembers Aijiro's horse' was first published in *Artemis*.

All other poems appear here for the first time.